# THE BRIGHT GAZE OF THE DISORIENTED

# THE BRIGHT GAZE OF THE DISORIENTED

Hubert Moore

Shoestring Press

All rights reserved. No part of this work covered by the copyright hereon may be reproduced or used in any means – graphic, electronic, or mechanical, including copying, recording, taping, or information storage and retrieval systems – without written permission of the publisher.

Printed by imprintdigital
Upton Pyne, Exeter
www.imprintdigital.net

Typeset by narrator
www.narrator.me.uk
info@narrator.me.uk
033 022 300 39

Published by Shoestring Press
19 Devonshire Avenue, Beeston, Nottingham, NG9 1BS
(0115) 925 1827
www.shoestringpress.co.uk

First published 2014
© Copyright: Hubert Moore

The moral right of the author has been asserted.

ISBN 978 1 910323 05 2

# ACKNOWLEDGEMENTS

For the title of this collection I am indebted to the Polish poet Wojciech Bonowicz and his translator, Elzbieta Wojcik-Leese, whose poem, *How to help,* I quote in translation and in full:

Once in a while a poem
raises its head.
Then you think

how to help it
retain the bright gaze
of the disoriented.

Acknowledgements are also due to the editors of the following: Dreamcatcher, Equinox, The Interpreter's House, Modern Poetry in Translation, New Internationalist, The North, Other Poetry, Oxford Magazine, Rialto, Scintilla.

*Phoning from Clapham* appears in *Visa Stories: Experiences between Law and Migration, The Ultimate Rendition* in the Amnesty anthology, *Fire in the Soul, 100 poems for Human Rights,* edited by Dinyar Godrej, *Murmuration for Eddie* and *To the man who picked my pocket on the 149* in *Canterbury Festival Poem of the Year (2013).*

# CONTENTS

| | |
|---|---|
| Sunflowers | 1 |
| Rasus | 2 |
| Compost poem | 3 |
| Boy's name | 4 |
| Afghan in London | 5 |
| Phoning from Clapham | 6 |
| Letter to Siberia | 7 |
| Exile | 8 |
| Uproot | 10 |
| Paving-stones | 11 |
| At a weekend of shearing | 12 |
| In place of a junction | 13 |
| Seaside photograph | 14 |
| Newness | 15 |
| Missed call | 16 |
| What the Lune saw | 17 |
| Fifth of four | 18 |
| Murmuration for Eddie | 19 |
| Water-happening | 21 |
| Inside story | 22 |
| To the man who picked my pocket on the 149 | 23 |
| Following lorries | 24 |
| Doorsills | 25 |
| Approaching the border | 26 |
| After 209 | 27 |
| Under oppression | 29 |
| To an interpreter from a country at war | 30 |
| Disclosure | 31 |
| Mining a silence | 32 |
| The ultimate rendition | 33 |
| Drone | 34 |
| The rule of the river | 35 |
| At Grenen | 36 |

| | |
|---|---|
| After a storm | 37 |
| At the Chinese Cemetery | 38 |
| De Bello Gallico | 39 |
| Kramm's iambics | 40 |
| Three poems for Hubert Pearson | 42 |
| To my fellow scrummager | 44 |
| Signing up | 45 |
| Footsteps | 46 |
| On the stairs | 47 |
| Buzzard | 49 |
| After a concert | 50 |
| In praise of rowing | 51 |
| Expedition | 52 |
| Marsh Harrier | 53 |
| Return to normal | 54 |
| Watering | 55 |
| Hosing down | 56 |
| Modes of dismissal | 57 |
| Heron ending | 58 |

# SUNFLOWERS

    for Haymanot

Adam and Eve they must be.
There's the requisite snake; and the ground
is littered with windfalls – apples,
for instance, juicy-looking and red,
and this single body of two
human beings, its shared shoulders,
its huddle of three or four knees,
all two hands of it clasping.

Heads would be useful of course
but Adam and Eve in this painting
don't have heads but sunflowers
which follow you round as though
you, dear viewer, were the sun,
you the moving spirit in this,
the light that conjured the artist's
colour and passion and wit.

# RASUS

My first shave left me scraped
smooth as an egg. And as crackable.
I was brand new, I was Humpty Dumpty
teetering on his wall.

Walking with the others
down the dark lane to chapel – winter,
stars still glittering – I felt
God's cool breath on my chin.

Things happen so nearly. What
if He'd breathed a bit harder, more coolly
still? If he'd spotted
the tabula rasa of me and made me

irretrievably His? If
I'd fallen off?

# COMPOST POEM

for Lief

You built us a frame to make compost.
You measured, sawed planks, hammered,
and three neat bays emerged. Myself,
I couldn't help thinking of cubicles,
the ones we each of us had at school
at the head of our beds: thirty of them,
all the way down our dormitory.

More like twenty probably. Things
get bigger and more: the muscles
the fair-haired boy who slept at the end
on the right used to let us touch;
beloved unhappiness smuggled each night
from the seat-box inside our cubicles
into our beds to be comforted.

But we didn't, I'm sure. Or not much.
More like took, used, poured, piled stuff
on to a heap, life-size, not over-
imagined at all: the cores and skins
of whatever we found to love, slow-
to-rot stalks of envy, the grounds
of being, still in a thick black sludge.

Layered and mixed and moist,
the compost of what has become of us.

# BOY'S NAME

The wooden post in the pond
where the kingfisher perches
is a bare post, and indeed
when they asked you your name
you couldn't say anything.

You knew it of course. You'd answer
if somebody said it. Kingfishers
come back, they don't abandon
their ponds. Look, it's there
staring into the water.

You lost everything, home, family,
country. How did you bring
that totally warm smile
through immigration? Or did it come in
hanging under a lorry?

So much is closed down now,
barricaded on the narrow streets
of your memory. It would be good
if, in its quite un-English plumage,
there on its post was the kingfisher.

But it's not. There's only a post. Enough
that your lost name – its kingfisher
colours I still can't really pronounce –
flits between blackened houses
and comes laughing back to you.

# AFGHAN IN LONDON

*for Stephanie*

Sleep longs for him.
It leaves its door wide open.
It waits for him in his favourite places.

But he rides past.
Can't glance, can't even think the live-wire
thing he knows, the live-wire thing that knows him.

All night
his bicycle whirls him on, whips
the spinning top of him to a pitch

too high-screaming
to hear the men when they came
to his father's house. The men when they come.

# PHONING FROM CLAPHAM

for Jade

I know you, how you skimp,
how you sit through a winter evening
without food, without heating, without
even a reading lamp.
I know you, your hunger,
your hurt anger, how your words,
rumpled after their journey,
tumble out of the telephone

and crouch in the warmth you send,
not on a page or screen
but an ironing-board in Uganda
where the school uniforms
of your almost orphaned nieces
have learnt to iron themselves,
to give themselves perfect creases.

# LETTER TO SIBERIA

We have arrived and have been well received.
The eel-grass on the North Kent mudflats
is as luscious and plentiful as we hoped.
When the tide is out we spend hours here
paddling, gobbling, muddying.

There are dangers of course, we keep watch.
We are one, the four or five hundred of us,
that is our saving: we waddle together,
we keep a sense of each other
as we did on the flight out.

But this isn't Siberia. Here,
when we make our small pleasure-words,
they say we are gargling. At best
we are curiosities: people ask
Are we pale-bellied or dark-bellied?

As for the sea, when the tide comes in
and we rest on its luke-warm slop,
our goose-flesh longs for the cutting
glitter of home and we ride
at not quite ease, not quite anchor.

# EXILE

> version of a poem by Noshin Shahrokhi translated from Farsi
> by Nasrin Parvaz

Two decades of it
have threaded ways
to lie unnoticed
in crevices, in wrinkles
across the forehead,
in smiles, in frowns.

Trust taste-buds
to remember. In unripe
nectarine or sour
red pomegranate seeds
a father's arms
are cradling a child.

Long lost, long preserved
that childhood: the clinging
scent of jasmine
keeps it sealed between
the almost never opened
pages of a book.

Inside the folds
of the hearing, a hatchet
sobs to shed the blood
of a tree, a mother's voice
is saying, *Come, your father
will die. I will die.
For the last visit, come.*

Everything chain-sawed back,
not only shoots that used
to spring so hopefully
but the root-stock stump
they sprang from.

# UPROOT

Tree-tops are way above me but from where
I stand, I think my staunchest, most
deep-rooted tree is leaning slightly
over.

Maybe my tree is stretched taut
as ever between tap-roots
clamped to juicy underground
and the suck of light.

Maybe it's me that's leaning. All I know
is a root which in its lazy
lightning struck out sideways
years ago

has shrugged away its topsoil, burst
into air, arching, rising up against.

# PAVING-STONES

    for Bridget

The quake came
and left your paving-stones
uprooted, tilted out of true.

Best, when you kneel
to lay them flat again,
to keep their equanimity,

their weight, their breadth, their calm
at the door of your mind,
so, when you come out

through it, when you leave
your still untilted house
walking on their broad backs,

you walk out on the true,
upright, unquaking.

# AT A WEEKEND OF SHEARING

You remember the sheep, don't you,
the flock we passed when you came
on Friday evening, how they
stood at the edge of their field
and gazed out from deep in the wiry
tangle of their winter wool,
how they gazed back at us?

And then – maybe it's lost, maybe
your illness cuts away all this –
us, after the warmth of our time,
driving home past the same field
on Sunday afternoon and almost
not recognizing them, how clean
and skinny they'd gone back to being

and how startled. Do you remember
you said you could feel them trembling?

# IN PLACE OF A JUNCTION

for Diana

Your nightmare route to work and back
is gone. Everything's changed,
even the map, the lay-out.
You wouldn't recognize it.

There's a new roundabout,
no T-junction, no queue to turn
right into the queue on the major
road, no inching out and across.

You'd whirl round it. Coming home
was always easier of course:
indicate left at the junction,
turn. The car remembers every

gear-change, every switch you touched.
Sometimes, approaching the roundabout,
on the long featureless curve
where the junction no longer is, it

still indicates. Doesn't actually
turn; nods though to roadside blackness
where the dead used to queue.
Saplings grow there now.

# SEASIDE PHOTOGRAPH

A sharp-featured man, the potter, Bernard Leach,
is wearing a dark suit,
collar and tie and hat. He's walking across the beach

when, in mid-stride, it happens. He stops, plants his umbrella
like a stake to fame
a yard off in the sand, and rigs himself up as a

cranky bipod, legs apart, one hand a table-top,
on which he coaxes
into salty air a sketch of the new: a bowl, a cup.

# NEWNESS

'only grief permits newness' (Walter Brueggmann)

I think you would have to grieve
totally, without thought, without purpose,
let alone without hoping
that newness would somehow follow,

to grieve up spring or hairy tassels
as tears for a weeping willow

or light or morning or love

or some such unthinkable shape
to fit an existing hollow.

# MISSED CALL

for Jane

You phoned just after you hadn't quite
seen an osprey. Your friend saw it. You
went back to the car and while you were gone

a small white hovering Christ must have come,
its claws demurely tucked and a harness
across its shoulders of huge dark wings.

I've not seen ospreys either. Which is good –
good for hoping, I mean, good for believing.
Please phone, love, when you miss an osprey again.

# WHAT THE LUNE SAW

for Marla Leichtmann

At long last, suddenly, after hurtful caging –
nowhere to spread your osprey span
of wings, to be full-stretch you – every village

in Cumbria grants you its freedom,
every view of distant lake or fell
opens up to you, every gleam

of river greets you back as one
of its own, its beloved. Three months
since a wide-eyed river, the Lune,

spotted you and a friend on its bank
not watching for ospreys at all
but noting kingfisher, redshank, greenshank,

and then while your friend was fetching
something left in the car, it
happened (only the Lune was watching):

no more than a swooping glance, I guess,
from osprey to human being, but a
quite translatable message – Yes,

ospreys, kingfishers, all, they would take good
care of you when you came to them,
feisty, spirited, one of their brood.

# FIFTH OF FOUR

The strange thing is
that we're so comfortable
out here, so much at ease

in this, Coach Five
of four the overhead insists
our train's comprised of.

We must be caught
up in a tent of air
behind Coach Four, a thought-

pocket, a fifth if not
a seventh heaven where
we're in a story yet

outside it: the firing-
squad has got us in its sights
and here we are desiring.

# MURMURATION FOR EDDIE

Was it that white-skyed, black-skyed
Friday evening we saw
the spectacular Mexican wave
starlings do before roosting
 when you Eddie?

Hundreds, maybe a thousand
black leaves in a leafless tree,
multi-twittering, multi-chattering, then,
as if on command, a single
silent voice. While you Eddie. While we

gaped at the smoke of them
gusting across the valley, one plume
of bird, wafting, swirling, twisting.
While you Eddie in your top-floor flat,
single-minded now in the last of the light.

Were they taunting, only
seeming to leave? Scatter of grit
thrown off, then whirling upward and round
and back, into their plumages, burnt
black on the cold white of the sky.

One smoke-in-the-wind thing,
starlings that Friday evening when
multi-talented you Eddie,
multi-active, multi-spirited, multi-caring,
ended your single life. No use

asking why, what wired these brains
to their act. You're gone and we,
however adept we are at not
missing each other too grievously,
miss you Eddie, miss you.

# WATER-HAPPENING

for Roger

I actually saw it happen:
you opened the stream and the water
followed its nose down the channels
you'd drawn in the dust and found
the roots of your fruit-trees,
your plums, your precious greengages.

You'd had the idea, you'd planned
and planted and channelled:
your poem was written and now
it was holding its cup to the place
where your roots come to drink,
it was lifting your branches,
filling the veins in your leaves
with a leaping green.

# INSIDE STORY

*for Nasrin Parvaz, who spent 8 years of the 20th Century in prison in Tehran and several weeks of the 21st Century in a London hospital*

We want you to come and visit
as soon as you're out. We want you
to see how the river divides
and flows through our city in ribbons,
in black almost underground (bundled
you into a car that was cruising
for this) streams. You'll love these

streams when you're out. The current
combs the waterweed, runs its fingers
through long ringleted hair. One morning
we'll go to a cafe where the only
music is water gurgling
past at your feet (you were strong, you
never gave in to their beatings).

I don't know how the streams (eight
of your years they took from you) find
each other again, how the river
remembers its single self, its old
blind-happy way. All I know (you took
yourself in for these latest seizures)
is we need your strongest flow to be now.

# TO THE MAN WHO PICKED MY POCKET ON THE 149

Dear thieving man,
I guess in the blur of all your split-
second snatchings you don't remember me,
once you'd spotted my pocket, I mean,
and the tip of the brown leather wallet
inside it, not quite snugly.

Let me remind you.
You got on the 149 at Dalston Junction.
Perhaps it's your patch, perhaps you always do.
My stop would be Shacklewell Lane.
I turned to the window to look.
You couldn't believe your luck.

Five or six times since then
I've used you, stolen you for my story:
how the bus stopped, drawing open
its doors for you; the crash of your exit;
you side-stepping through shoppers; my pocket
inside-out and empty.

So, thieving man, we're accomplices,
you and I. I start again and again
at Dalston Junction. You do too – how,
in broad daylight, this man
on the bus was staring out of the window,
pocketing people's stories.

# FOLLOWING LORRIES

If in your heart-high car
(the head won't do, no haughty
Defenders or Guardsmen),

rather than cruising at 80
down the middle or outside lane,
you watch for a gap and indicate

and slip in left between the sheer
face of one lorry
and the ramrod back of another,

you can almost see into
the cavity, eye-crawl through
to the fierce low place

where, in egg-shell skulls,
young men's stories are hatching
to the howl of wheels.

# DOORSILLS

Not ramparts, not trenches,
not frontiers even, barbed fences
keeping armies from armies,

but, fierce as guard-dogs,
doorsills in their millions,
each at its angle marking
the new front line: where
lintels know not to lower
the blunt axe of themselves
to less than an inch of each
stooping homecomer's head; where stone
plumps its cushion to suit
a child's, a mother's, a grandmother's
widening haunches; where clickety
latches open up to the flip
of a known forefinger or voice
but are jammed to intruders.

Not that the frail new front
doesn't splinter inward
at the first kick of their boots.

# APPROACHING THE BORDER

He crossed into Uganda, she into Greece,
certain young men went into and out of Iran.
Nothing ended here, nothing began.

Only a language: one kicking open
the door of another one's
concepts, naming, naming, making silence

talk. Even then these people
crossed no border. The long lines of their past
waited inarticulate, jostling.

# AFTER 209

The original Farsi version of this anonymous poem appeared on a website in Iran after the arrest of students taking part in a peaceful demonstration. Ward 209 of Evin prison, Iran, is where prisoners are taken for interrogation and torture. Literal translation from Farsi was provided by Nasrin Parvaz.

It must be good, you say,
to have our children back
from 209. How are they?

We can't answer. We have words
enough but so light-weight,
whittled to such smoothness

we can't tell. Rather ask
the children themselves. Listen
to them, they've brought home

new-fangled ways of speaking.
Hear the raw gap that finds
its tongue in Keyvan's mouth.

Listen to Elnaz, her right
leg blurting out the livid
thing they did to it. How's

Nasim? Nasim's trembling
goose-flesh tells and tells
its story, can't draw breath.

Rozbeh can't stop either,
can't not tap what happened
happened happened on his knee.

Anosheh weeps and doesn't
weep and weeps: weeps words,
weeps silences that speak.

Don't miss the unblinking
testimony of Mohsen's
eye-lids, how fluently

they stutter; or that of
Mehdi's forehead, its frank
statement, its in-your-face

insistence. What about
Behrooz then, who had a
perfect fore-arm once that

couldn't speak? Hear now its
eloquence. Hear words
our children bring from 209.

# UNDER OPPRESSION

At night they sit with their feet
in the coldest water they can,
these two from hotbed Sudan.

The sky where they sit
is a milk of blackness and stars.
Till late in the early hours

they mutter poems to each other.
The click of their tongues
booms in the milky water, longs.

# TO AN INTERPRETER FROM A COUNTRY AT WAR

Beating, burning, killing:
you know the men's stories

almost before they tell them.
Tender-to-hear home-language

comes to your door in London,
the hearing room of your head.

English equivalents, they're
no problem. Translation, though,

is an echo that howls back,
loudspeaks grief of your own.

# DISCLOSURE

As bread makes
beneath kind white muslin,
I want you, dear stranger, to have
as long as it takes

for stories
of untellable shame
to swell with your last few grains
of love for yourself and rise.

# MINING A SILENCE

> Churches at Lalibela in Ethiopia are carved out of the landscape rather than built with brick or stone or wood

When that first evening you phoned
and couldn't say anything, silence
was there already, under
the slope of the hill. The men –
some say the Holy Ghost had rolled
up its sleeves and was digging too –
had opened an Ethiopian hill
and were finding the church inside it.

So, back here, I sat on the edge
legs dangling into the hollow
and waited not for your voice to come up
clogged with holy African rock-dust –
it was much too early for that –
but for silence to breathe.

# THE ULTIMATE RENDITION

is
to find a word
of quiet dignity, impeccably
connected (music, literature),
that will ask no questions
and will stop at nothing
(not the sending

of a man
by plane across a sea
to somewhere else, so somewhere else
can torture him and we don't have to)

and make it seem
a mild necessity, it happens,
it's rendition,

like the sea's gesticulations,
wrenching, heaving upward
as the plane comes over,

like dread
that trickles coldly down the spine,

like handcuff-sores, like sobs.

# DRONE

I kill, that's the point of me.
Any one, any where.
I'm totally single-minded:
no heart, no qualms, no conscience.

And no names mentioned.
When I'm sent on a mission
I go, but it isn't
the sender who sent me.

No casualties either.
I'm a blessing, I bring
home no body-bags,
none of the mess of blame.

And you don't have to wait
for a war to send me droning.
I kill cleanly, peacefully.
I must be an act of God.

# THE RULE OF THE RIVER

"We do best, I think, when we write what happened to us." (Rasul Akele)

Those workshop evenings,
though we worked the same river,

you'd come headlong towards us
letting turbulence carry you
on its back, all rapids
of pain, rapids of laughter,

and we'd be labouring through
our placid water. Denting it,
going deeper, sending churnings
scuttling downriver behind us,

we'd paddle away at what never
actually happened, while you
swirled past on your tide
of almost unwriteable happenings.

# AT GRENEN

*to a young refugee writer*

Wish you were here, we write,
and you are, at the northern tip
of Denmark, where two seas meet:

where the North Sea and the Baltic,
as though each was the other's
antithesis, leap back

at the difference, white
at white upthrown. Yet where the rocks
end, on the point, a street

of land wades out and we all –
especially you, pen poised,
in London, in the two minds

of your need – go shoes in hand
through crashing rainbow sky
and stand with a foot in each sea:

the thunder and thunder of now,
its fists, its long thin fingers
stealing across your page;

and what you remember, that thunder.

# AFTER A STORM

By morning
casualties have arrived:
multiple loose weepings are lying
under the willow.

All night the tree has listened.
Now it dips its root
into the black of the pond
and writes.

# AT THE CHINESE CEMETERY

"It prescribes a silence of what has been happening, it forces people to make-believe that nothing, in fact, has been happening." (Ariel Dorfman)

Every silence
is a silence of what has been happening,
a still
of juices warm from their events.

Ask what death
young men from China died in Northern France
in 1917,
the fields breathe only their breath.

*A Good Reputation endures for ever*
is all.
Misty stillness clings to a row of poplars
beside what might be a river.

# DE BELLO GALLICO

Tunnelling down through the trees
from some hill-fort in France
where the Romans defeated the Gauls
or the Gauls the Romans

we flush out mothy things
that nestle there, work
loose the locals, switch them on
like head-lights in the dark:

startle a great white owl.
It beats thick air, blunders
along ahead of us down
the hole through the trees;

can't break out into open
untunnelled sky, can't go slow
till we've passed. Bangs into branches,
comes De Bello Gallico

blindly down into now –
where what we're thinking is this:
conquest never forgets,
runs in our veins ahead of us.

# KRAMM'S IAMBICS

Did the bell ring? Did we call to him?
I can't remember. What I hear
and hear is the rhythmical bounce
of Rev. Heinz Herbert Kramm
down the stairs from his attic bedroom
to an English wartime supper.

Two steps, one light, one thuddingly
accented taking the Pastor's
weight; then two steps more, ker-
Kramm, two more, two more. These were
my first iambics, first refugee,
first person from Germany.

What did my father and mother mean
taking him in, feeding him,
letting him not wash up? They even
talked in German with him. *I must
jump away,* he said when he'd finished
his food, and they let him.

We tried our best, my brother and I,
for the allies, for us. What
we wanted was victory, wasn't it,
total dominance. We filled
his bicycle bell with gravel,
air gushed from his tyres.

Iambics, though, have lodged in my head
ever since: the thud, the thud, the thud
of coming downstairs to join us,
of nothing absolute, nothing
without conditions, men being men,
enemies not being enemies.

# THREE POEMS FOR HUBERT PEARSON

1.

The sky is thick with us:
coming down, landing,
the Jeremys, the Elizabeths, the Hughs.

The Huberts even. My namesake, thirteen
years before me, gives
at the knees as the earth

gives at the knees to receive him.
Comes, I guess, in loving
memory of some

previous Hubert, much-missed uncle-to-be,
still young perhaps when he drowned
in an earlier sea:

carries the candle for him,
carries his quivering name.

2.

I've been advancing for 63 years
up through Belgium, up through Holland,
and I know Lieutenant Pearson

will be holding the bridge when I come.
He has been assured that the relieving army
will work its way up to Arnhem

if the First Airborne Reconnaissance Regiment
can capture and hold the bridge.
Well, they've done it. At this moment

I am staring down into the Rhine.
All I can do is honour.
Leading his men into action

Pearson died. I hereby re-name
myself after him, for him.

3.

On white museum bikes we ghost
through woods near Arnhem, where once
airmen eclipsed the sky. Even

the trees round here have fallen
on their feet, legs slightly bent,
relaxed. No brakes, we pedal

backward to remember
how, ruddy with hope, with cause,
the ripe parachutes fell.

Branches droop with their weight.
No wonder we're white
underneath them: our parents

used colours for their grief,
their great-hearted wars.

# TO MY FELLOW SCRUMMAGER

for James Stearns

You, my easy to bind with, easy
to laugh with, dear dead friend,
took the right, I seem to remember,
while I was left. And we never
stopped mocking each other.

In scorn, in friendliness
you never missed a trick:
poured your disdain on the disgraceful
views I took from my favourite
paper. 'Guaardian,' you'd drawl.

I wasn't far behind you:
I'd put two age-long 'a's
in 'Telegraaph'; between its lines
I'd slip in all my dis-
affection, all my affection.

In two hundred scrums maybe
we pushed as one together:
arm-locked, your left arm round
my waist, my right round yours,
shoulder to shoulder, bound.

And now not only I
but all of us who knew you
throw out our right arm for the sense
of you being bound to us:
your voice, your laugh, your kindliness.

# SIGNING UP

    for Lawrence Sail

I wanted to say
we've been friends for 52 years
and how good.

But the sea
doesn't count on its fingers of spume
the times it races up beaches.

And the land
makes no mention of blessings,
let alone issues annual statements.

So I didn't try.
I'd have floundered, I'm sure,
out of my depth in sentiment.

What I did
was surf about in the shallows,
and when you signed with Avaaz
to stop the circumcision of women,

I signed too.
Did you see me there, four seconds behind you?

# FOOTSTEPS

*for Elinor*

Waiting for news, for a blessed call
to say my child, her mother's
daughter still, is now
a mother herself,
I might as well

watch blackbirds
hopping weightlessly across
the bristle of my new-mown grass,
three or four hops, stop,
three or four more, toward

the grandmother
of all twisted willow-trees,
who, though she seems too gnarled to care,
spins round to catch them at it.
They freeze, just happen to be there.

# ON THE STAIRS

The injured man drags himself
               of his story.
   up the stairs
back

From the waiting-room you can see him
               his fist
     through the past,
wrenching up

gripping the banisters.
               memory,
     each precipitous
Each step,

he is nearer to having no head.
         another:
     leads to
One thing

to have been in so wrong a place
         makes nothing
at so wrong a time

of heads in the end. And only
       up from there
a step or two

he'll have no upper body either.
      is for him
All I want

to walk at large and whole
on the first floor
in the present tense.

# BUZZARD

How to make her happy?
We sit at the edge of the woods
while, hundreds of feet above us,

the great buzzard of her
searches about in her grief.
Doesn't hover: prowls, soars, circles,

leaves no stone of the shocked
self unturned, the pale stone
that the mouse or rabbit or vole

makes of itself in the searchlight
stare of a buzzard, or the pebble
holding its breath which might turn out

to be happiness crouching there.

# AFTER A CONCERT

It must have been the ecstatic
applause of the audience
that turned the head

of the music stand
the first violin had been using.
We could see,

when the stand's turnabout
finished up in our faces, straight
into the score,

like seeing
*Arrangement enabling human beings*
*to experience happiness*

scrawled, wrong way up,
on a cloud or old envelope.

# IN PRAISE OF ROWING

You square your oars
and push the flat of them
flat through the dense
coherency of water.

You drive each oar's-worth
spinning back towards
the time you first dipped in
too deep, too splashily.

You get the rhythm
and you do this simple
cursive thing. You can't
of course look forward,

follow some fixed intention
marked up on your
horizon. All you can do
is gaze the length

of all the froth behind you,
re-read it as it settles.
Where can you go
but on from what you've written?

# EXPEDITION

When grief came, he went:
went slowly down to the shore,
took the boat, took the oars
and watched as the mainland
lost its edges, eased,
softened to mist or sea.

Way offshore, island
rasped up underneath him. He
climbed it, found he could whittle
the dead wood of aloneness.
His mountain of single self
rose sheer from the beaches.

Not that he couldn't leave, line
his mountain up, send
rowed water swirling back
to the island. He crossed, went ashore:
there was no one to grieve,
nothing had kept but her name.

# MARSH HARRIER

A dream of water and a reed-bed
got him thinking, Could he raise
(*If you have to be sure,* John Berryman said,

*don't write*) a spirit from it? Could
the skulking genius of the place –
a dream of water and a reed-bed

and the power of doubt were all he had –
be so believed in that it rose
(*If you have to be sure,* John Berryman said)

from its marsh and flew or glided
low across us at a sort of ease?
A dream of water and a reed-bed

opened cloudy eyes and so did
mud and doubt and, very nearly, sureness.
*If you have to be sure,* John Berryman said.

*Can you see? Marsh Harrier.* He pointed.
Long tail. Long wings. Flight almost languorous.
*If you have to be sure,* John Berryman said,
stay in your dream of water and a reed-bed.

# RETURN TO NORMAL

    for Alick Moore

Watching you do your summoning,
your conjuring up
of jay, marsh harrier, waxwing
from their shady places,

it seems that as you walk
your territory – garden, reed-bed,
woods – your ramrod
wordlessness

is how to do the hardest
easiest thing, allowing.
Jay, marsh harrier, waxwing
hang on your will

for when
a million years of caution
end and they come gliding back
into our company.

# WATERING

Pleasure's a brilliant way, I know,
to keep us to our job
of propagating

but I want it pure:
I want to dip the can
and take a weight and depth

of pondwater each evening,
not the raddled glitter
in the glare all day

but going deeper
for the cooler blacker stuff
from up a creek

where, if you watch,
the sun slips shivering in
without its clothes on,

then pour it back and see it
plunge into itself again,
leaving the plants unwatered.

# HOSING DOWN

You might be lucky. You might
be on the 17.24 from Waterloo
to Charing Cross and happen
to be glancing left precisely when
a gap between two buildings
rumbles past with two hard-hatted
men in it, also a mixer
which has finished mixing, a
crusted wheel-barrow and spades.

This can't be willed of course.
It's pure luck if, as you pass,
it happens one hard-hatted man
is at that moment hosing
clean the other's wellington
boots. Don't miss the care he gives,
the way he stoops and comes
in at an angle and the other
lets him do it, trusts him.

Trains come past any minute here
especially at rush hour, the time
for slowly stopping work. You
might be lucky if you took
the 17.21 or 17.28 and happened
to glance left and see the other,
in a gap of what seems happiness
between before and after,
hosing the first one's boots.

# MODES OF DISMISSAL

for Sam

My new garage-man said my car
had the air (he'd always thought
LBW was a dodgy mode of dismissal)
of a car that's uncared for.

Did I ever, he asked (bowled,
caught, stumped even), check
(he knew where he was with them)
the oil, the water? LBW, though –

how can a man come
to godlike conclusions like that?
Can a person make, on however
insightful a whim,

the merely probable true?
My garage-man, though, could see
through the steel walls of a car.
I was plumb in front. He knew.

# HERON ENDING

When what seems like an ending
comes to you, when you find

yourself standing on the far
side of some sort of water

glaring back at it, when there's no
question of spearing any more

fish, you grapple up, your front
as always too heavy. You beat

stiffly off. Nothing remains
to be left fiercely unsaid.